Love You For a Liar

Zen Collins

Presentation by *BookLeaf Publishing*

Web: www.bookleafpub.com

E-mail: info@bookleafpub.com

ISBN: 9789357696913

First edition 2022

DEDICATION

I dedicate this to everyone who hasn't made their way into my work - trust me, it's a compliment.

Otherland

A motherless motherland
We watched the sky come down in pieces
Drawn to shreds by a will we couldn't reason with
The children fell silent
And a father on the borderline reaches for a family beyond
his grasp
The world waits
On its soapbox
offers pocket change for its own comparative peace of mind
And pledges little more than allegiance in colours.
If we closed our eyes
We could remember the music
And the laughter of the lives we'd once known
And know better than to reach for a world that expected us
to cower from the eastern star.
And sometimes I wonder
If I feel anything but a faint tremble as the earth shakes
from rows of tin soldiers toppling
But I pray I'll never know the barbed wire against my skin
The panic in the streets
And the cold nothingness that follows.

Soho Is for Lovers

I wonder if part of me still lies
Fragmented
In the leather of your mother's passenger side
Dreaming of the day when the last we'd see of this place
Would be the view from the rear-view mirror
Looking forward to eternity through the gaps in our fringes.

I wonder if part of me still lingers
With Hawthorne Heights on the stereo
Or the sweat in our palms
Playing Thelma and Louise
Or the back roads we took
Trying to avoid congestion charges.

Does part of me still fall asleep
Counting your freckles
Or do I loiter in my own memory
That night
Somewhere under Chinatown?
Perhaps that is why I still see flashes of floral wallpaper
And little glimpses of us in the mirror
All black tears
Black denim
My name on your wrist in black marker
And the sound of the speakers against a closed door
And as I think of my last look at you
Tripping over your laces
I wonder
Would part of me ever repeat
Whatever words sent you away.

Kill Your Darlings

Kill your darlings; or merely wish them away
With every half-hearted prayer
You fell to your knees and called upon the false idols you
held so dear
Questioned the power you'd given them
By the gold of their hair
Thrown yourself before them; adored them - adored Him
For He was not man nor mortal.
Some claimed Him an angel;
A test, a trick – a trap
Fallen, haloed
Sheltered amongst the bastard children that so became Him
Tugging on their wings
Begging for a shred of dignity we'll never afford them.

Kill your darlings; or let them get away
To live a life of solitude rarely glancing at the shelf
where He'd kept but one page dedicated to you
Swept away between friends and foes and lovers
Acquaintances and strangers and brothers
All the same to Him.
The bringer of end times was He
The giver of life, the original sin
Your redemption.

Kill your darlings; for they serve you no more
In vino veritas, He taught you the ways of the world.
You'd begun to grow weary
For He was a different man with every bottle.
You were disillusioned with the champagnes you couldn't
pronounce

And the friends who vanished into the walls.
You become his masterpiece
A disaster, piecing together the shards of the curls and
pearls of pretty girls
He wouldn't give the time of day.
Another line in a stanza
Engraved with 'run, boy, run'.

Kill your darlings; and immortalise them with words
Place them, case them, keep them safe.
You were a river, a stream
Or just a drop to quench a thirst
So kill your darlings
Before they get you first.

White Picket Fence

Somewhere we're still here
Behind that white picket fence
With such status symbols we clawed our way to
something more than this.

But there was never a life past this
Suburban sprawl
Not in dreams nor driveways
And so we sojourn
Somewhere amongst smiling wives and stepford lives
Just waiting for an out.

It wouldn't have mattered to me
If not for the way the lights in our eyes dulled
Behind cut and paste plasterboard
How your spark began to fade
I watched you slip away
To something else
Moulded by matrimony.

And still my mind wanders
To thoughts of your morning coffee
The faint smell of bitter almonds
An acrid taste on the tip of your tongue
But I'm drawn back to my reality
Of washing machines
And long nights
Listless

Inhaling carbon monoxide
Cinnamon scented from the gas oven.

So shielded by delusions
Or dreams of a life on the outside
We make it through day by day
We waste away
Behind that white picket fence.

Columbia

I told my therapist about that night
Like she could help me find meaning in my own motives
and indiscretions
Or take away the thought of how your eyes
A hazy shade of cosmic
Opened slowly as if I'd pulled you out of your sophomore
slumber.
I feigned nonchalance at you
Perched on a bar stool
Mimicking a beatnik you'd seen in a movie
Swirling a Cabernet like you were even 21
But fought past your freshman groupies
And tried not to meet your gaze in the middle of your
glasses
Met you halfway
Traced the lines on the High Fidelity poster in your
bedroom
Traced your smile from dimple to dimple with my finger
And tried not to feel out of place flowing you though
Williamsburg
Maybe intimidated by your aura
So urbane
Effortless
And the lais sez faire of your Brooklynite manner
Still, it was hard to feel so bad
Watching your face glow as you talked about Pinkerton
Or those meaningless conversations
About dreams and fears and Fenders
Brunch, breakdowns, Buzzcocks and benders

I had a handle on it,
Until we basked in the twilight
And you told me how you cried yourself to sleep the night
of your Bar Mitzvah
And from there you became a hideaway
A release for a resentment I cannot quantify
You tossed your hair out of your eyes
And slid my bracelet further up your forearm
Inked a few lines up mine that I scrubbed raw in the
afterglow.

Elephant

We don't need to talk about
Little rows of wooden crosses
Or the pathetic reality that your lungs'll give up on you
before I do.
We don't have to talk about national headlines
Or hours of interrogation and swearing I knew nothing.
We don't need to talk about whys or consequences.
We don't have to talk about anything.

Not testimonies, eulogies
Or sobbing in the bleachers.
Nor cheerleaders who've seen too much
Or what's become of teachers.
The winos in the parking lot
Who drown the whole thing out
Or empty goddamn corridors
And 'reasonable doubt'.
And I won't try to rationalise
Or analyse you, kid.
'Cause we don't need to talk about
What it was you did.

Gaslights

I'm sick to death of you
Sobbing in the corner, like you didn't provoke me.
I think about the lines on your face and if I'm bored with you
Or how happy we could be if you weren't so difficult, and you didn't fight me.
You.
You make me a bastard.
It's alright – I'll just tell you you're beautiful
And you'll love me again.
That I couldn't go on without you
That my world would cease on its axis
And you'll eat it up.
Graze it, like cattle.
If you decide you're going again, I'll remind you what happened the last time
And how it was all your fault.
Warn you that the last word trailing off my dying breath will be your name.

I don't mean it, obviously
But you wouldn't know that – would you?
I can shred you to pieces, dice you like an onion
And you'd fall to your knees and beg forgiveness.
I can sleep knowing I've kept you up, with a thousand thoughts of what you did wrong tonight
What you do and don't deserve.
And how you'll have to smile and keep it shut tomorrow
Because you don't want them to get the wrong idea, do you?

And listen to me darling, darling
They could never understand what we have.
I can turn on the gaslights
Or I could shut you in the dark.

And you know it all too well, honey
That every word that leaves these lips is poison
That I am pure venom
And I am seeping through your veins.

You Sick Beauty, You

You were born in the Upper East Side
And spent your life resenting it.
I met you on a bathroom floor in the city
With your school tie as a tourniquet around your forearm
Head lolling, swiping your hand over a lighter
Desperate to feel anything.

Now I check your pulse every half hour or so.
You're someone else when you're not breathing right
Someone good, maybe.
Your face is translucent, your eyes roll back
You've convinced yourself you're a higher power
Tormented yourself with martyrdom.
I could feel sorry for you if I tried.

Trying not to look at you
Because I know you thrive in adoration.
You're sat there, centre of attention as always
With a perm and an attitude like you're Lou Reed
Cigarette hanging off your lips
Words dripping manufactured angst
But I know your eyes like nobody else
Bloodshot
Hidden behind aviators
Shielding the sanguine from a night sobbing into my
pillows like the little boy I met on that bathroom floor
Shrouded in your sycophants
Messianic
But you'll remember me when your novelty's worn off
And reach for me, catatonic
Vanish long before the morning comes.

I wish only for the apathy that so becomes you
Fashionably blasé
Brooding, Byronic
Dreaming of life in the gutter
So far removed from your world of trust funds and
townhouses
And unwilling to accept your worth, as I have mine.

I am an afterthought
A pave in the sidewalk, perhaps
Whilst you are a star on the boulevard.
You sick beauty, you.
And like Pierrot at your court, I am but your fool.

The House in Belladonna

You'd headed up north once there was nobody left to stay
for
Made a life for yourself over the years
And you hadn't so much as dreamed about going back to
the house in Belladonna
But here you were.
It wasn't as though you'd made a conscious decision to
come back
You'd simply boarded the train a day ago, in a state of mind
you couldn't quite explain
Somehow wound up on a platform in Atropa County, and
resolved to walk the rest.

You weren't certain how long you'd been walking
Somewhere along the way you'd dumped your suitcase,
and clung instead to a hip flask like an infant
Taking swigs with increasing frequency as the reality of
where you were going started setting in.
You knew you were getting close when you ran out of road
And all signs of life were a distant thought.

Not so much as a breeze, or a bird chirping
It should have been dilapidated beyond recognition
Yet you knew every last crevice of the place.
You reached the old churchyard, now a mass of bramble
And memorials for people nobody had thought about in
years.
Your mood blackened with the thoughts of every last
funeral procession.

You closed your eyes and listened out for the lingering
chimes of the church bells
And the faint drawl of a preacher, prophesying eternal
damnation
But nothing came.

As you continued through the town you once called home
It all came flooding back, and at once you felt immersed in
your youth.
Days spent wandering the town with little intention
Avoiding the glare of the old voodoo woman out on her
veranda
Swiping at the air to keep the sun out of your eyes.
The two of you, hand in hand through the grounds
Euphoric, back when the roses were still in her cheeks.
The magnolias you plucked and set in her hair, while she
smiled at the sky and counted the clouds
And tossing dimes into the stream, wishing for the world.

Your mind skipped over a couple of years, to when they'd
put the fear of God into her
And so her hand fell limp in yours
Or pulled away altogether, as she shrunk out of your grasp.
At night you heard her weep and murmur in her sleep, 'til
they carted her off and kept her in a room somewhere you
couldn't see her anymore.
You didn't like this part.
You didn't want to think about it.
But as you approached what remained of the house in
Belladonna
Your mind was filled with ailing relatives and bloodstained
handkerchiefs
Lonely nights in an emptying house, desperately clinging to
its former glory

And singing dirges for dead girls you watched waste away,
buried in the wedding dresses they never had a chance to
wear.

At some point you'd made your way in, slipped in through
a broken window
And found yourself confronted by soiled portraits in rusting
frames of the ancestors you'd abandoned
Then the nausea hit you and the urge to flee again.
You knew you could go, leave your old homestead to
shrivel up and die.
Or you could stay, clamber through the ruins of the
ballroom, and dance with the ghosts of everyone you ever
loved.

Amber Alert

If you're dead, it's just for the hell of it
Or you just wanted a reason not to return my calls.
I stopped caring by the seventh year
But they're still leaving flowers by your photograph
And lighting candles to 'guide you home'
'Cause you're so damn precious.

If you're dead, you're an angel.
God love you for a liar
Hiding in your medicine cabinet
My magnum opus.
And all that remains of you
Is that sweet smile
A sick smirk in the picture on every lamppost in town.

If you're dead, you're loving this.
Wherever you are
Watching everyone adore you.
You brought the suburbs to their knees
Black tears to powdered cheeks
They're holding out
Hoping
Waiting
But to me you're just another dead girl
Illuminated in the soft glow of an amber alert.

The Last Line is the Hardest

If you'd taken me that night
I'd have called you the rapture
Still, I convulse at the sound of your name.

And if I could look past my own loathing
I'd want you in my final hours
Because I'd give you every day I have
For just the feeling.

I'm not naïve enough not to know
That the last line is the hardest
But I've resigned myself to waking up in cold sweats
And a relief that never comes.

If you'd taken me that night
I'd have called you the saviour
Because I'd let you destroy me
If you'd just get me out of my head.

To Be Beside The Sea

It felt like hours since we'd stopped talking
It couldn't have been that long
We hadn't even reached the pier yet
But it was dark already, and the chips had turned stale
Which I thought was fitting.
You started tossing them to the seagulls
Even though you knew they terrified me
Or maybe because you knew.
I could never be too sure.

You tried to break the silence eventually
Parroting some joke you'd read on the promenade last
summer
And I didn't even crack a smile.
That set you off alright, and a fine mess we were for the
tourists
Sat al fresco at the greasy spoons, now getting dinner and a
show.
It didn't matter
I couldn't hear you over the howling of the wind
Though I might have cried if not for all the salt in my eyes.
We must have stopped at some point
Because our audience went back to pondering their battered
sausages
And I was realising that it would take a lot more than a 99
flake
And cheap scampi to fix us.
That maybe it wasn't just the weather
It was you.
It was all you.

I wanted to scream that in your face
Or just walk into the sea and never look back.
But instead, I took your hand and strolled alongside
Praying to be washed away by the tide.

Portrait of an Artist

His mind divine
He sits across the room
Shrouded in some hand-me-down
Threadbare
Hunched over a notebook.

His fingers are numb
Skin peeling
Brittle boned
He nurses a wound from a guitar string
But says nothing of the marks on his arm.

I'd call him deluded
If not for his genius
Sat in that studio
Poverty as performance art
Whilst his inheritance grows.

And I know he doesn't need me anymore
For he long since found a darker muse
And so engulfed by Her beauty
He starts to decay
Some kind of hypodermic hero
He dreams of adoration
And prostrates himself at the altar of Her influence.
It would never be enough for him
I see his face, pained, stained
That slight limp in his walk he'd never explain

But I'm not his saviour
And he'd never stop
Until he meant something
Anything.

An ATM on Park Avenue

I was at an ATM on Park Avenue when it occurred to
me
That I was born into a generation ravaged by
Affluenza
The sickness is our birth-right
Passed down by fathers who themselves inherited
ennui and a lack of interest in the futures that had
been bought for them
Unexceptional in all but heirlooms

It was at this ATM on Park Avenue
That I saw my reflection against the Bank of America
And looked past myself in my grandmother's pearls
Pressed the prongs of my ring into the palm of your
hand to see if you'd feel anything
Stopped to check my lipstick in the window of a town
car
Toasted to boredom in the backseat
And watched the world as we went past with an
upturned nose

I caught their eye somewhere around Madison
And fell into your crowd
All faux fur 5th Avenue
And long drags from cigarettes they'd started
smoking out of au pair's purses
Trading ambition in solid gold for the affection
they'd chased in the early years

Confined to the perimeters of prep schools
Defining themselves by family crests

I wanted to know the feeling
Maybe I already did
I told myself I was different
That they were something I'd read in a book
Or in a movie I'd aspired to some time ago
But I was at an ATM on Park Avenue when it
occurred to me
That I wanted so much more.

Bittersweet Sixteen

I gave up searching for anything resembling a purpose by
my thirteenth year
Found it in plastic cups and cigarette butts by bittersweet
sixteen.
I could have wanted the world
But I linger beyond
Content in my world of histrionics
Gazing into the Pandora's box I unleashed upon my youth.

And I don't want to think about destinations,
I don't want to find God.
We cared about nothing but divinity
Virginity
Adoration.
I smile for miles
In clouded minds and kitten heels
Somewhere between scarlet lips and self-abasement.

I was destined for bigger
Better
But I'll stay here
Whistle the small-town blues
Drowned out by girlish cacophonies
And dreams of being anybody.

Père Lachaise

The 32nd was the beginning of the end for us
When I looked at you
A synecdoche for all I've ever adored
And felt nothing but an apathy
Or thoughts trailing off as your voice withered my
consciousness
With your fixation on such vanities as your own mortality
Like the time you called me from Père Lachaise
Lying on Jim Morrison's grave
Weeping something incomprehensible
Maybe French
But Beautiful.
Still I'm taken over by a burning indifference
Or a desire to accessorize myself with someone new
But I see you in the whites of my eyes
You grip me by the irises
And I count myself to sleep on your heartbeat
It's better that than lie awake
And wonder if I should keep you
Just a wrinkle on the portrait in my attic.

Venus in Neverland

Our humanity runs red in the gutter
Like the water I left you in that night
Where I skipped stones and counted seconds as you
bled out.
I'm almost sorry for you
But I loved you only as an idea
My own immaculate conception
Your eyes once silver fade to gray.

Now your name's on every station
And millions mourn for friends and family who will
never see
Your dark roots fade to gray.
Your image is venerated
Your bedroom floor consecrated ground.
But you're a false idol
A fake clairvoyant trying to read my mind
You wouldn't like me so much if you could.

You mistook me for your someone you could care
about
But I can't hide the cruelty in my eyes.
I am nothing more than the monster under your bed
A changeling child in the photos on your mantle
The cold shoulder your parents weep upon
Something infernal waiting in your bedroom window
To take your hand and lead you into the night
Swore I'd take you to paradise.

Your scent engulfs me
Perfume and peroxide
My skin burning hot as jazz against yours
Colder
My favourite word is 'why?'
And I never found an answer
If you'd only take my hand we could fly away
And you'd be Venus in Neverland.

Flores Para Los Muertos

She came to me every year
And though I worshiped her like my God, I couldn't
take her hand.
Bowing at her alter
Begging for just another year
I offered up scapegoats wrapped in marigolds
Sacrificed Abuelos who didn't have much longer
And she stole them away into the dark.

No one wants to die, not really
That's what I told myself each year
Desperate
Decrepit
Hollow, I raise a blade
Watch the leaves of a family tree once proud, once
noble
Drop and wither away in the fall
And tear away a fragment of myself, as I listen to
every last plea
Watch the light go out in their eyes
Grant her every wish in exchange for a life I can't
bear to live
Santa Muerte, save my soul.

I fall to my knees
Heart ravaged by thoughts of children torn from their
mothers' arms
Blood of lovers come and gone stains my hands

Seeps into my skin
Becomes a part of my very being.
Weeping in the mirror
Searching for a reflection
Only a monster stares back
Gagging, praying to anyone who'll listen
Howling in aguish on the graves I dug with my bare
hands
Santa Muerte, let me go.

I have to live with myself
And my mind
Or at least whatever remnants of a conscience
remains
In this joyless calaca you leave behind
The faces just a flicker in the corner of my eyes
Weaving in and out of my consciousness
Their voices shrieking
My fate sealed, I sojourn
Alone
With no choice but to listen
Santa Muerte, take me away.

And I'll never meet my maker
For I long ago shed the shell He put me in
Traded in the very essence of my humanity
Santa Muerte, save my soul.

In Absentia

I left my heart somewhere along the way
Searching every street in every city
For a year after you disappeared.
So don't tell me I didn't try.

I'm sat here in the dark
With only the madness you left me
And your old spoils for company.
Your life was a concept album
Your very being so defined by who they thought you were.
So don't tell me I didn't try.

You drowned me in your cheap liquor
Filled me with your poisons.
You don't fool me.
I could whittle you down to a splinter
Embed you in my skin
So you could never go away again.

I miss you.
I miss it all.

Every night in the ambulance.
Every siren.
Every last gasp before the room goes dark.
Every time you 'died' in my arms.

You could have told me what I did wrong.
Or given me something more than the melancholy
And nights spent asking the picture in my wallet;
Where did you go?

An Episode

Could be 24 hours
Could be 5 minutes.
Like Sarah Kane at 4:48
With nothing but a pair of earbuds to hold it together.

Tracing your arm
Begging yourself not to.
Filled with a loathing you can't rationalise
Lying there, motionless
As it grips you by the throat and drags the air out of
your lungs.
Letting it feed on you and thrive.

Or fifteen minutes in the mirror
Finding faults that won't be there when you're
thinking straight.
Blinking away tears, eyes stinging
Collapsing in on yourself to songs about the love
you'll never know.
Then festering in the dark
And just letting the episode play.

Ambien(ce)

I'm under your skin
Prop your head up every so often so they don't
suspect a thing
Reel you in and hold you back
Clinging to that cold stare.
I'm on your mind
Keep you mine with words and whispers
Sweet nothings and the stain on your sheets
Be forever your everything
And that dullness in your eyes.
I'm all you are
Breathe me in and let me out
To prey on your psyche
Keep you coming back
And make you understand
That you are nothing without me.
And you don't want to be free
You don't want their love
Their affection
Their voices drip with sanctimony
Their arms ephemeral
And my grip tightens

www.ingramcontent.com/pod-product-compliance
Lightning Source LLC
LaVergne TN
LVHW010951200726

843509LV00013B/2366